VEGETARIAN

1998 Published by Rebo Productions Ltd., London
Designed and created by Consortium, England

Typeset by MATS, Southend-on-Sea, Essex
Printed in Slovenia

Ceres Verlag recipes compiled and translated by Stephen Challacombe

Cover design by Minkowsky, Enkhuizen, The Netherlands
JO240 UK

Edited by Anne Sheasby
Illustrated by Camilla Sopwith

VEGETARIAN

Inspiring ideas for
delicious main meals, snacks and treats

REBO
PRODUCTIONS

Contents

Introduction

An ever-growing number of people are turning to vegetarianism for a variety of reasons - some out of concern for the well-being of animals, others for environmental reasons and many for health reasons.

Studies suggest that vegetarians are significantly less likely to develop cancer at an early age than meat eaters. Added to that, because vegetarians and vegans are often slimmer than meat eaters, eat more fibre and more complex carbohydrates in the form of wholegrain cereals, nuts and pulses and also eat fewer saturated fats (predominantly found in animal products), they enjoy lower levels of blood cholesterol and therefore heart disease and have a higher level of protection against several bowel diseases.

But besides offering a healthy diet, if well-balanced, vegetarian food provides the opportunity to enjoy a whole new taste experience beyond the confines of the traditional meal. This is the chance to exploit to the full the wealth of fresh and exotic fruits, vegetables and herbs now freely available all year round, as well as the heady mix of spices and flavourings drawn from the cuisines of the world. Then there are those all-important, nourishing staple foods which offer enormous potential for creating imaginative and delicious dishes - nutty grains such as couscous and wild rice, toothsome tomato and spinach-flavoured pasta, sweet nuts such as pistachios and pecans and tender pulses including flageolet beans and chick-peas.

This book presents a collection of exciting recipes for everyone who enjoys good food, whether they are committed vegetarians or not. Sample the vegetarian highlights of international cooking, such as Spanish Gazpacho soup, Greek Tzatziki dip, Indian Vegetable Curry and Middle Eastern Tabouleh salad, or savour the delights of some contemporary creations including Watercress and Mushroom Paté, Parsnip Fritters, Potato and Courgette Gratin, Chocolate and Almond Biscuits and Cashew Ice Cream. So, why not go vegetarian today!

Split Pea Soup

A classic vegetarian soup which looks extra special with a swirl of yogurt on top.

Preparation time: 10 minutes • Cooking time: 40 minutes • Serves: 6

Ingredients

225 g (8 oz) split peas

1.7 litres (3 pints) vegetable stock or water and a stock cube

55 g (2 oz) vegetable margarine

1 large onion, chopped

3 sticks celery, chopped

2 leeks, thinly sliced

2 medium potatoes, diced

1 medium carrot, finely chopped

Salt and freshly ground black pepper

Leek slices, to garnish

Method

1
Cook the split peas in the stock in a saucepan for 10-15 minutes, stirring occasionally.

2
Meanwhile, melt the margarine in a separate pan, add the onion, celery and leeks and cook for a few minutes, stirring occasionally.

3
Add to the peas and stock together with the potatoes and carrot and bring back to the boil.

4
Reduce the heat, cover and simmer for 30 minutes, stirring occasionally.

5
Remove from the heat and cool slightly, then purée in a food processor or blender until smooth.

6
Return the blended mixture to the rinsed-out pan and reheat gently until piping hot, stirring occasionally.

7
Season to taste with salt and pepper and ladle into warmed soup bowls to serve. Garnish with leek slices.

Serving suggestion

Serve with fresh bread or bread rolls.

Variations

Use green or brown lentils in place of split peas. Use sweet potatoes in place of standard potatoes. Use 1 parsnip in place of the carrot.

Cook's tips

If the vegetables are chopped small enough, you can serve this as a chunky soup. If you do not have a food processor or blender, you can press the soup through a sieve, although it will not be quite as thick.

Gazpacho

One of Spain's tastiest exports, this chilled soup makes an elegant starter.

Preparation time: 15 minutes • Serves: 4

Ingredients

450 g (1 lb) ripe tomatoes
1 small onion
1 small green pepper, seeded
1 clove garlic, crushed
1/4 medium cucumber
15 ml (1 tbsp) red wine vinegar
15 ml (1 tbsp) olive oil
400-g (14-oz) can tomato juice
15-30 ml (1-2 tbsp) lime juice
Salt and freshly ground black pepper
Croutons, to garnish

Method

1
Plunge the tomatoes into a bowl of boiling water, leave for 1 minute, then plunge into a bowl of cold water. Remove and discard the skins and seeds. Set aside.

2
Chop the onion and pepper and place in a food processor or blender with the tomatoes, garlic, cucumber, wine vinegar, oil and tomato juice

3
Purée until smooth and well mixed.

4
Add the lime juice and seasoning to taste and blend to mix.

5
Pour the soup into a glass dish, cover and chill until required.

6
Ladle into soup bowls to serve and garnish each serving with a few croutons.

Serving suggestion
Serve with lightly buttered wholemeal bread.

Variations
Use plum tomatoes or yellow tomatoes in place of standard tomatoes. Use 1 small leek in place of the onion. Use cider vinegar in place of red wine vinegar.

Cook's tip
If the soup is too thick, add more tomato juice after step 4.

Garden Vegetable Soup

A hearty mixed vegetable soup – perfect for those cold winter nights.

Preparation time: 15 minutes • Cooking time: 30-45 minutes • Serves: 4-6

Ingredients

15 ml (1 tbsp) margarine
½ head of fennel, finely chopped
3 medium carrots, diced
1 onion, chopped
2-3 cloves garlic, crushed
1 parsnip, diced
Salt and freshly ground black pepper
10 ml (2 tsp) dried parsley
15 ml (1 tbsp) tomato purée
1 large potato, diced
1.2 litres (2 pints) vegetable stock
55 g (2 oz) frozen peas

Method

1
Melt the margarine in a large pan and add the fennel, carrots, onion, garlic, parsnip and salt and pepper.

2
Cover and allow to 'sweat' over a very low heat for 10-15 minutes, stirring occasionally.

3
Add the parsley, tomato purée, potato and stock.

4
Stir well, bring to the boil, then simmer for 20-30 minutes, until the vegetables are cooked and tender, stirring occasionally.

5
Just before serving, add the peas.

6
Bring back to the boil and serve immediately. Ladle into warmed soup tureens to serve.

Serving suggestion

Serve with crusty rolls or slices of French bread.

Variations

If fennel is not available, use 2 or 3 sticks of finely chopped celery. Use sweetcorn kernels in place of peas.
Use 1 large sweet potato in place of standard potato.

Cream of Sweetcorn Soup

Serve this luxurious soup with fresh crusty French or Italian bread.

Preparation time: 10 minutes • Cooking time: 25-30 minutes • Serves: 4-6

Ingredients

30 ml (2 tbsp) olive oil
6 onions, sliced
6 corn on the cob
1 litre (1¾ pints) vegetable stock
90 ml (6 tbsp) double cream
Freshly ground black pepper, to taste
Freshly grated nutmeg, to taste
Chopped fresh parsley, to garnish

Method

1
Heat the oil in a large saucepan, add the onions and cook gently for 10-15 minutes, until softened, stirring occasionally.

2
Meanwhile, cut away the corn from the cobs with a sharp knife, working lengthways down each cob. Add the sweetcorn kernels to the onions with the stock and stir to mix. Bring to the boil, then reduce the heat. Cover and simmer for 10 minutes, until the sweetcorn is cooked and tender, stirring occasionally.

3
Remove the pan from the heat and cool slightly, then purée in a food processor or blender until smooth. Return the soup to the rinsed-out pan, add the cream, pepper and nutmeg and reheat gently until hot, stirring occasionally. Ladle into warmed soup bowls and serve garnished with parsley.

Mixed Vegetable and Barley Soup

A satisfying soup enriched with soured cream. Serve with bread rolls or oatcakes.

Preparation time: 20 minutes, plus overnight soaking time • Cooking time 20-30 minutes • Serves: 6

Ingredients

100 g (3½ oz) rye grains
100 g (3½ oz) pearl barley
200 g (7 oz) sauerkraut, thinly sliced
2 green peppers, seeded and sliced
1 leek, thinly sliced
2 sticks celery, thinly sliced
4 firm tomatoes, sliced
4 young carrots, thinly sliced
10 ml (2 tsp) salt
5 ml (1 tsp) fennel seeds
5 ml (1 tsp) chopped fresh tarragon
Freshly ground black pepper, to taste
100 ml (3½ fl oz) milk
100 ml (3½ fl oz) soured cream
15 ml (1 tbsp) chopped fresh dill

Method

1
Place the rye and pearl barley in a bowl and cover with cold water. Leave to soak overnight.

2
Place the prepared vegetables in a large saucepan with the soaked grains, soaking liquid and 500 ml (18 fl oz) water. Add the salt, fennel seeds, tarragon and pepper and stir to mix.

3
Bring to the boil, then cover, reduce the heat and simmer for about 20-30 minutes, or until the vegetables and grains are cooked and tender, stirring occasionally. Stir in the milk, cream and dill, reheat gently, then ladle into warmed soup bowls to serve.

Tzatziki

A classic and refreshing starter or snack.

Preparation time: 10 minutes • Serves: 4-6

Ingredients

500 g (1 lb 2 oz) cucumber

500 g (1 lb 2 oz) plain yogurt or crème fraîche

1 clove garlic, thinly sliced

30 ml (2 tbsp) finely chopped fresh mint

Olive oil, to taste

Salt and freshly ground black pepper, to taste

Fresh parsley sprigs, to garnish

Method

1
Cut the cucumber in half lengthways, then remove and discard the seeds and cut the flesh into small cubes. Place in a bowl.

2
Add the yogurt or crème fraîche and garlic and stir to mix well.

3
Add the mint, olive oil and salt and pepper and mix well.

4
Spoon into a dish and serve garnished with fresh parsley sprigs.

Serving suggestion
Serve with pitta bread, black olives and fresh vegetable crudités.

Variations
Use Greek yogurt if you like. Use chopped fresh mixed herbs in place of mint.

Cook's tip
The cucumber can be coarsely grated rather than cut into cubes.

Cheese and Pepper Bites

These colourful mini kebabs combine three different types of cheese with mixed peppers for an attractive and flavourful appetiser – ideal for a drinks party or buffet.

Preparation time: 15 minutes • Cooking time: 15 minutes • Serves: 3-6

Ingredients

1 yellow pepper
1 red pepper
1 green pepper
5 ml (1 tsp) olive oil
Salt and freshly ground black pepper
85 g (3 oz) vegetarian sheep's cheese
85 g (3 oz) vegetarian Gorgonzola
85 g (3 oz) vegetarian Gouda or Cheddar cheese

Method

1
Brush the peppers all over with oil, then place on a baking tray.

2
Bake in a preheated oven at 220°C/425°F/Gas Mark 7 for about 15 minutes, turning every 5 minutes, until blistered and brown.

3
Remove the peppers from the oven, cover with a damp cloth and allow to cool slightly.

4
Remove and discard the skin, seeds and cores from the peppers. Cut the flesh into strips, then season with salt and pepper.

5
Cut each of the cheeses into equal sized pieces. Place the sheep's cheese on the yellow pepper strips, the Gorgonzola on the green pepper and the Gouda or Cheddar on the red pepper.

6
Thread onto cocktail sticks or skewers and serve.

Serving suggestions

Serve with a mixed leaf or chopped salad or crusty bread.

Variations

Use 1 beefsteak tomato in place of the red pepper. There is no need to roast the tomato – simply remove the seeds and cut into strips. Use vegetarian Stilton in place of Gorgonzola.

Watercress and Mushroom Paté

A quick-to-make and delightfully light paté made with low-fat curd cheese.

Preparation time: 10 minutes • Cooking time: 5 minutes • Serves: 4

Ingredients

25 g (1 oz) butter

1 onion, finely chopped

85 g (3 oz) field mushrooms, finely chopped

1 bunch of watercress, finely chopped

115 g (4 oz) low-fat curd cheese

A few drops of shoyu (Japanese soy sauce)

2.5 ml (½ tsp) caraway seeds

Freshly ground black pepper

Lime wedges, to garnish

Method

1
Melt the butter in a saucepan over a low heat, add the onion and cook until soft but not coloured, stirring occasionally.

2
Increase the heat, add the mushrooms and cook quickly for 2 minutes, stirring frequently.

3
Add the chopped watercress and stir for about 30 seconds, until it becomes limp.

4
Place the contents of the pan in a food processor or blender together with the cheese and shoyu. Blend until smooth and well mixed.

5
Stir in the caraway seeds and pepper to taste.

6
Place in individual ramekin dishes or one large serving dish, cover and chill for at least 2 hours, until firm, before serving. Garnish with lime wedges.

Serving suggestion

Serve with thin slices of lightly buttered brown bread or toast.

Variations

Use fresh wild mushrooms in place of field mushrooms. Use rocket leaves in place of watercress. Use 4 shallots in place of the onion.

Cook's tip

It may be necessary to stir the contents of the food processor or blender several times, since the mixture should be fairly thick.

Marinated Beans

These dressed beans make a substantial vegetarian starter.

Preparation time: 15 minutes, plus soaking and marinating time • Cooking time: 1½ hours • Serves: 4

Ingredients

200 g (7 oz) mixed brown and white beans
1 sprig of fresh thyme
500 ml (18 fl oz) vegetable stock
2 whole cloves
1 onion
2 cloves garlic
1 bay leaf
Fresh herb sprigs, to garnish

For the dressing

1 onion, sliced
Sea salt, to sprinkle
2 cloves garlic, crushed
2.5 ml-5 ml (½-1 tsp) Dijon mustard
2.5 ml- 5 ml (½-1 tsp) dried oregano
60 ml (4 tbsp) red wine vinegar
75 ml (5 tbsp) olive oil
1 bunch of fresh parsley, finely chopped
Freshly ground black pepper, to taste

Method

1
Wash the beans and place in a bowl. Cover with water, add the thyme sprig and leave to soak overnight. Drain.

2
Pour the stock into a pan and add the beans.

3
Press the cloves into the peeled onion, then add the onion, garlic and bay leaf to the stock and beans. Stir to mix.

4
Bring to the boil, then cover, reduce the heat and simmer for 1½ hours, until the beans are cooked and tender, stirring occasionally.

5
Strain through a sieve or colander and reserve the beans. Discard the stock, onion and garlic.

6
Meanwhile, for the dressing, place the onion in a bowl and sprinkle with sea salt. Leave for 10 minutes to allow the salt to be absorbed.

7
Add the crushed garlic to the onion with the mustard, oregano, wine vinegar, oil, parsley and pepper to taste.

8
Mix the dressing with the beans, cover and leave to marinate in the refrigerator for several hours before serving. Serve, garnished with fresh herb sprigs.

Serving suggestion

Serve with garlic bread.

Variations

Use wholegrain mustard in place of Dijon mustard. Use walnut or hazelnut oil in place of olive oil. Use fresh basil in place of parsley.

Mixed Nut Balls

This versatile dish can be made in advance and refrigerated until required for cooking.

Preparation time: 20 minutes • Cooking time: 20-25 minutes • Serves: 8

Ingredients

60 g (2¼ oz) ground almonds
60 g (2¼ oz) ground hazelnuts
60 g (2¼ oz) pecan nuts
85 g (3 oz) fresh wholemeal breadcrumbs
115 g (4 oz) vegetarian Cheddar cheese, grated
1 egg, beaten
60-75 ml (4-5 tbsp) dry sherry or 30 ml (2 tbsp) milk and 45 ml (3 tbsp) dry sherry
1 small onion, finely chopped
15 ml (1 tbsp) grated fresh root ginger
15 ml (1 tbsp) chopped fresh parsley
1 small red or green chilli, seeded and finely chopped
1 medium red pepper, seeded and diced
5 ml (1 tsp) sea salt
5 ml (1 tsp) freshly ground black pepper
Lemon or lime slices, to garnish

Method

1
Mix the almonds, hazelnuts and pecan nuts together with the breadcrumbs and cheese in a bowl. Set aside.

2
In another bowl, mix the beaten egg with the sherry, onion, ginger, parsley, chilli and red pepper.

3
Combine with the nut mixture and add the salt and pepper. Mix well.

4
If the mixture is too dry, add a little more sherry or milk.

5
Form the mixture into small 2.5-cm (1-in) balls.

6
Arrange the balls on a well greased baking tray and bake in a non-preheated oven at 180°C/350°F/Gas Mark 4 for about 20-25 minutes, until golden brown. Serve warm or cold, garnished with lemon or lime slices.

Serving suggestion

Serve on individual plates on a bed of chopped lettuce. Garnish with slices of lemon and hand round your favourite sauce in a separate bowl.

Variations

Use ground walnuts in place of pecan nuts. Use 1 shallot in place of the onion. Use 1 yellow or green pepper in place of the red pepper.

Bulgur Boats

This attractive snack makes a conveniently portable dish for picnics.

Preparation time: 15 minutes • Cooking time: 20 minutes • Serves: 4-6

Ingredients

55 g (2 oz) green lentils

115 g (4 oz) bulgur wheat

1 red pepper

1 green pepper

1 onion

55 g (2 oz) pine nuts (dry roasted in a pan)

10 ml (2 tsp) dried salad herbs (tarragon, chives or parsley)

Rind and juice of 1 lemon

Salt and freshly ground black pepper

4-6 Cos lettuce leaves, to serve

Wedges of lemon, to garnish

Method

1
Remove any grit or stones from the lentils and rinse well.

2
Place in a pan, cover with plenty of water, then bring to the boil and simmer for about 20 minutes, taking care not to overcook.

3
Meanwhile, place the bulgur wheat in a mixing bowl and cover with boiling water. Leave for about 10 minutes – the grain will then have swollen, softened and absorbed the water. Drain off any excess water.

4
Seed and dice the peppers and finely chop the onion.

5
Drain the cooked lentils and add to the bulgur wheat, together with the peppers, onion, pine nuts, herbs, lemon rind and juice and salt and pepper to taste. Mix well.

6
Using one large lettuce leaf per person, spoon the bulgur wheat salad into the centre of the leaves and arrange on a large serving dish garnished with wedges of lemon. Serve.

Serving suggestion

Serve with fresh crusty bread.

Variations

Use cashew nuts or peanuts in place of pine nuts. Use 15-30 ml (1-2 tbsp) chopped fresh mixed herbs in place of dried herbs. The bulgur mixture could be served in 'parcels' of lightly blanched cabbage leaves.

Cook's tip

If the salad is not required immediately, cover and refrigerate until required.

Chinese Cabbage Gratin

A delicious cheese-topped mixed vegetable bake.

Preparation time: 20 minutes • Cooking time: 30 minutes • Serves: 4

Ingredients

750 g (1 lb 10 oz) Chinese cabbage

250 g (9 oz) mushrooms, sliced

Salt and freshly ground black pepper

150 g (5½ oz) crème fraîche

150 g (5½ oz) full cream plain yogurt

2 medium eggs

Grated nutmeg, to taste

Curry powder, to taste

100 g (3½ oz) mature vegetarian Gouda cheese, grated

Method

1
Cut the Chinese cabbage into four and rinse thoroughly. Cook in a saucepan of salted boiling water for about 6 minutes.

2
Drain the cabbage, then place it in a greased ovenproof dish.

3
Lay the mushroom slices over the cabbage and season to taste with salt and pepper.

4
In a bowl, mix the crème fraîche and yogurt together, beat in the eggs and season with salt and pepper.

5
Add grated nutmeg and curry powder, stir well, then pour the sauce over the mushrooms.

6
Sprinkle with the grated cheese and cook in a preheated oven at 200°C/400°F/Gas Mark 6 for about 30 minutes, until golden brown. Serve hot.

Serving suggestions

Serve with a mixed leaf salad or baked potatoes.

Variations

Use courgettes in place of mushrooms. Use vegetarian Cheddar cheese in place of Gouda. Use green cabbage in place of Chinese cabbage.

Potato Nests

An ideal supper dish and an excellent way of using up leftover potatoes.

Preparation time: 15 minutes • Cooking time: 20-25 minutes • Serves: 2

Ingredients

1 onion, finely chopped
450 g (1 lb) potatoes, cooked in their skins
A little milk
A knob of butter
Salt and freshly ground black pepper
2 medium eggs
25 g (1 oz) vegetarian Cheddar cheese, grated
Chopped fresh parsley, to garnish

Method

1
Cook the onion in a little water in a saucepan until softened. Drain.

2
Peel the cooked potatoes and mash in a bowl with the milk, butter and salt and pepper to taste.

3
Add the drained onion and mix well.

4
Divide the mixture in half and make 'nests' on a greased baking sheet.

5
Crack an egg into each nest and sprinkle with grated cheese.

6
Bake in a preheated oven at 200°C/400°F/Gas Mark 6 for 20-25 minutes, or until the eggs are set. Serve, garnished with parsley.

Serving suggestions

Serve with beans and grilled tomatoes or a salad.

Variations

The nests can be filled with chopped leftover nut roast mixed with a mushroom or tomato sauce and a few freshly chopped herbs. Use sweet potatoes in place of standard potatoes.

Parsnip Fritters

These tasty fritters make a nice change for a light lunch or snack.

Preparation time: 10 minutes • Cooking time: 5-8 minutes per batch • Serves: 4

Ingredients

115 g (4 oz) plain unbleached flour

10 ml (2 tsp) baking powder

5 ml (1 tsp) salt

2.5 ml (1/2 tsp) freshly ground black pepper

1 medium egg

150 ml (1/4 pint) milk

15 ml (1 tbsp) melted butter

700 g (1 lb 9 oz) cooked parsnips, finely diced

Oil or clarified butter, for frying

Method

1
In a bowl, sift together the flour, baking powder, salt and pepper.

2
Beat the egg in a small bowl and mix with the milk and melted butter.

3
Stir the egg mixture into the dry ingredients.

4
Stir in the cooked parsnips and mix well.

5
Divide the mixture into 16 equal portions and shape into small fritters.

6
Heat the oil or clarified butter in a frying pan. Fry the fritters in batches until browned on both sides, turning occasionally. Serve hot.

Servings suggestions

Serve with yogurt sauce or make them slightly larger and serve as a main course with salad.

Variations

Courgettes, sweetcorn, onions or aubergine can be used in place of the parsnips.

Indonesian-Style Okra

An interesting vegetable dish of okra, tomatoes and onions flavoured with fresh parsley.

Preparation time: 15 minutes • Cooking time: 25 minutes • Serves: 4-6

Ingredients

1 kg (2 lb 4 oz) okra
45 ml (3 tbsp) spiced vinegar
30 ml (2 tbsp) olive oil
2 onions, thinly sliced
10 tomatoes, skinned and chopped
Salt and freshly ground black pepper
45 ml (3 tbsp) chopped fresh parsley
500 ml (18 fl oz) vegetable stock
Fresh parsley sprigs, to garnish

Method

1
Top and tail the okra, then blanch in a saucepan of boiling water for about 3 minutes.

2
Place the okra in a colander, sprinkle with vinegar, then drain well and set aside.

3
Heat the oil in a frying pan, add the okra and onions and cook until the okra change colour and the onion softens, stirring continuously.

4
Add the tomatoes, salt and pepper and parsley to the pan, then add the stock.

5
Bring to the boil, cover, then reduce the heat and simmer for 10-15 minutes, until the vegetables are cooked and tender, stirring occasionally.

6
Serve hot, garnished with fresh parsley sprigs.

Serving suggestions
Serve with warm ciabatta or oven-baked potatoes.

Variations
Use sesame oil in place of olive oil. Use fresh basil in place of parsley.

Mushroom Dumplings with Creamed Spinach

An unusual yet satisfying dish of mushroom-flavoured dumplings served with spinach enriched with quark and crème fraîche.

Preparation time: 25 minutes • Cooking time: 30 minutes • Serves: 4-6

Ingredients

30 ml (2 tbsp) butter
2 onions, thinly sliced
225-g (8-oz) can mushrooms
15 ml (1 tbsp) Cognac
2 cloves garlic, thinly sliced
90 ml (6 tbsp) chopped fresh parsley
175 g (6 oz) plain flour
About 250 ml (9 fl oz) milk
125 ml (4 fl oz) double cream
30 ml (2 tbsp) finely chopped shallots
15 ml (1 tbsp) green peppercorns
300 g (10½ oz) fresh spinach leaves
15 ml (1 tbsp) olive oil
Salt and freshly ground black pepper
250 g (9 oz) quark (low-fat curd cheese)
150 g (5½ oz) crème fraîche
Fresh herb sprigs, to garnish

Method

1
Melt the butter in a pan, add the onion and cook until softened, stirring occasionally.

2
Drain the mushrooms, finely chop, then add to the pan. Cook for about 5 minutes, stirring occasionally.

3
Add the Cognac and 1 clove garlic. Increase the heat and cook until the juices in the pan are reduced, stirring frequently.

4
Stir in the parsley, remove the pan from the heat and set aside to cool.

5
In a bowl, mix the flour with the milk and cream, then stir in the mushroom mixture, shallots and peppercorns.

6
Mould the mixture together and form into dumplings.

7
Cook the dumplings in a saucepan of salted, boiling water for 10-15 minutes. Drain well and set aside to cool.

8
Meanwhile, wash the spinach and cook in a saucepan with the olive oil without adding any water until wilted. Drain well and squeeze out any excess water. Chop the cooked spinach.

9
Add the remaining garlic and season with salt and pepper to taste.

10
Allow the spinach to cool, then mix with the quark and crème fraîche.

11
Serve the dumplings with the creamed spinach alongside. Garnish with fresh herb sprigs.

Servings suggestions

Serve with a mixed leaf salad or crusty French bread.

Variations

Use broccoli florets in place of spinach leaves and boil for 5 minutes until tender. Mash well before adding the remaining ingredients. Use canned sweetcorn kernels in place of mushrooms. Use chopped fresh basil in place of parsley.

Cauliflower and Broccoli Souflettes

Serve this dish as a winter-time snack or as a main meal with rice salad and ratatouille.

Preparation time: 25 minutes • Cooking time: 35 minutes • Serves: 6

Ingredients

350 g (12 oz) cauliflower
350 g (12 oz) broccoli
55 g (2 oz) vegetable margarine
55 g (2 oz) brown rice flour
425 ml (¾ pint) milk
55 g (2 oz) vegetarian Cheddar cheese, grated
1 large egg, separated
A good pinch of ground nutmeg
Salt and freshly ground black pepper

Method

1
Break the cauliflower and broccoli into small florets and steam over a saucepan of boiling water for about 7-10 minutes, until just tender.

2
Melt the margarine in a pan, remove from the heat and gradually add the flour. Stir to form a roux, then add the milk gradually, blending well to ensure a smooth consistency.

3
Return the pan to the heat and stir until the sauce thickens and comes to the boil. Remove from the heat.

4
Cool a little, then add the cheese and egg yolk. Stir well and add the nutmeg.

5
In a bowl, whisk the egg white until stiff, then fold carefully into the sauce.

6
Place the steamed vegetables into 6 small buttered ramekin dishes and season with salt and pepper.

7
Divide the sauce evenly between the dishes and bake immediately in a preheated oven at 190°C/375°F/Gas Mark 5 for about 35 minutes, until puffed and golden. Serve at once.

Serving suggestion
Serve with a mixed green side salad.

Variations
Use courgettes and mushrooms or baby corn cobs in place of cauliflower and broccoli.
Use vegetarian Parmesan cheese in place of Cheddar.

Mixed Grain Patties

These tempting, crispy snacks are fragrantly flavoured with fennel and served sprinkled with grated cheese.

Preparation time: 15 minutes • Cooking time: 15 minutes • Serves: 2-4

Ingredients

350 g (12 oz) quark (low-fat curd cheese)
200 g (7 oz) plain wholemeal flour
5 ml (1 tsp) salt
Freshly ground black pepper, to taste
Grated nutmeg, to taste
1 bunch of spring onions, finely sliced
1 bulb of fennel, sliced
175 g (6 oz) wheat grains, cooked
175 g (6 oz) pearl barley, cooked
50 g (1¾ oz) sunflower seeds
About 50 g (1¾ oz) vegetable margarine
100 g (3½ oz) vegetarian Emmenthal cheese, grated

Method

1

Drain the quark thoroughly. In a bowl, mix the quark with the flour, salt, pepper, nutmeg and prepared vegetables.

2

Mix the wheat grains and pearly barley with the sunflower seeds and add to the quark mixture. Mix well.

3

Heat the margarine in a frying pan, then add the grain mixture. Spread out over the base of the pan and fry for about 5 minutes, until it has formed a crust, then turn and fry the other side until crispy.

4

Break apart with 2 forks and fry the pieces for a further 2 minutes. Sprinkle with the grated cheese to serve.

Serving suggestions

Serve with a mixed dark leaf salad or a mixed pepper, tomato and onion salad.

Variations

Use pumpkin or sesame seeds in place of sunflower seeds. Use white flour in place of wholemeal flour. Use vegetarian Cheddar cheese in place of Emmenthal.

Red Lentils with Vegetables

This tasty combination of red lentils and vegetables makes a warming and filling main course dish.

Preparation time: 15 minutes, plus overnight soaking • Cooking time: 45-60 minutes • Serves: 4

Ingredients

400 g (14 oz) red lentils
30 ml (2 tbsp) olive oil
2 cloves garlic, crushed
1 onion, cut into small chunks
1 carrot, cut into small chunks
1 leek, cut into small chunks
1 stick celery, cut into small chunks
30-45 ml (2-3 tbsp) tomato purée
650 ml (22 fl oz) vegetable stock
30 ml (2 tbsp) white wine vinegar
1 sprig of fresh thyme
Salt and freshly ground black pepper
A pinch of cayenne pepper
30 ml (2 tbsp) honey
1 bunch of fresh chives
Slices of leek, to garnish

Method

1
Wash the lentils thoroughly under cold running water, then drain well. Place the lentils in a bowl, cover with water and leave to soak overnight.

2
Heat the oil in a pan, add the garlic and cook until softened. Add the prepared vegetables and cook briefly, stirring.

3
Stir in the tomato purée and stock, then bring to the boil.

4
Drain the lentils thoroughly, add to the pan and stir well. Cover and simmer for 30-40 minutes, until the vegetables and lentils are almost cooked and tender, stirring occasionally.

5
Stir in the wine vinegar and thyme. Season with salt and pepper and cayenne, then stir in the honey.

6
Continue cooking over a moderate heat for a further 10-15 minutes, stirring occasionally.

7
Meanwhile, finely chop the chives, leaving a few leaves whole for garnishing.

8
Once the dish is cooked, adjust the seasoning and serve sprinkled with chopped chives. Garnish with slices of leek and whole chive leaves.

Serving suggestions

Serve with French bread and a green salad or cooked fresh vegetables such as broccoli and carrots.

Variations

Use green or brown lentils in place of red lentils. Use chilli powder in place of cayenne pepper. Use fresh parsley or basil in place of chives.

Spaghetti Pasty

An impressive wholemeal pasta pie, filled with a delicious carrot, mushroom and tofu mixture.

Preparation time: 45 minutes • Cooking time: 30-45 minutes • Serves: 4-6

Ingredients

300 g ($10^{1/2}$ oz) wholemeal spaghetti
1 kg (2 lb 4 oz) carrots, sliced
4 medium eggs, beaten
45 ml (3 tbsp) crème fraîche
45 ml (3 tbsp) cornflour
1 clove garlic, thinly sliced
30 ml (2 tbsp) chopped fresh basil
15-30 ml (1-2 tbsp) soy sauce
Salt and freshly ground black pepper
30-45 ml (2-3 tbsp) sunflower oil
500 g (1 lb 2 oz) button mushrooms
200 g (7 oz) tofu, cut into small cubes
400 ml (14 fl oz) milk
Ground nutmeg, to taste
125 g ($4^{1/2}$ oz) vegetarian Cheddar cheese
Fresh herbs sprigs, to garnish

Method

1
Cook the spaghetti in a large pan of boiling salted water for about 15 minutes, or until al dente. Rinse with cold water, drain well, then lay out flat on a board so that the spaghetti does not stick together. Set aside.

2
Meanwhile, steam the carrots over a pan of boiling water for about 30 minutes, until very tender. Purée the carrots in a food processor or blender until smooth.

3
In a bowl, mix the carrots with 3 eggs, the crème fraîche and cornflour. Stir the garlic into the mixture with the basil, soy sauce and salt and pepper to taste. Set aside.

4
Meanwhile, heat 15 ml (1 tbsp) oil in a pan and fry the mushrooms with a little salt for about 5 minutes, until the liquid has evaporated, stirring occasionally.

5
Add the mushrooms and tofu to the carrot mixture, stir well, then set aside.

6
Beat the remaining egg, then coat the spaghetti thoroughly in the beaten egg.

7
Line an ovenproof dish with cooking foil and brush with some of the remaining oil.

8
Arrange some of the spaghetti on the dish in spirals against the edge of the dish. Spoon in the carrot mixture and press so that the spaghetti is held firmly in place against the sides of the dish. Top with the remaining spaghetti, then cover with cooking foil that has been coated with the remaining oil.

9
Bake in a preheated oven at 220°C/425°F/Gas Mark 7 for 30-45 minutes, until cooked.

10
When cooked, remove the foil, carefully remove the pasty from the dish and remove the foil from underneath it. Place on a serving plate and keep warm.

11
Meanwhile, for the cheese sauce, pour the milk into a pan and season with salt and pepper and nutmeg. Add the cheese and cook gently, stirring continuously, until the sauce becomes creamy and is hot.

12
Serve the spaghetti pasty with the cheese sauce alongside. Garnish with fresh herb sprigs.

Serving suggestion

Serve with cooked fresh vegetables such as green beans and sweetcorn.

Indian Vegetable Curry

A wonderfully tasty curry which has the added advantage of freezing well.

Preparation time: 20 minutes • Cooking time: 1 hour 40 minutes • Serves: 4

Ingredients

10 ml (2 tsp) ground turmeric
5 ml (1 tsp) cumin seeds
5 ml (1 tsp) mustard seeds
5 ml (1 tsp) fenugreek seeds
20 ml (4 tsp) coriander seeds
2.5 ml (½ tsp) chilli powder
5 ml (1 tsp) ground ginger
5 ml (1 tsp) black peppercorns
450 g (1 lb) onions, finely chopped
About 60 ml (4 tbsp) vegetable oil
300 ml (½ pint) sterilised milk
30 ml (2 tbsp) white wine vinegar
400-g (14-oz) can tomatoes, liquidised with their juice
15 ml (1 tbsp) tomato purée
10 ml (2 tsp) brown sugar
5 ml (1 tsp) vegetable bouillon powder or 1 vegetable stock cube dissolved in a little boiling water
900 g (2 lb) chopped mushrooms or mixed vegetables such as mushrooms, cauliflower, carrots, potatoes and okra

Method

1
Grind all the spices together using a pestle and mortar. This amount will make 45 ml (3 tbsp) curry powder. Set aside.

2
In a saucepan, fry the onions in the oil until golden, stirring occasionally.

3
Add the ground spices, lower the heat and cook for 3 minutes, stirring continuously.

4
Add the milk and vinegar and stir well.

5
Add the liquidised tomatoes, tomato purée, sugar and stock.

6
Bring to the boil, cover and simmer gently for 1 hour, stirring occasionally.

7
Add the vegetables and cook for about 30 minutes, until tender, stirring occasionally. Serve.

Serving suggestion

Serve with boiled brown rice, chappatis and cucumber raita made by combining diced cucumber with plain yogurt, a little chopped fresh mint, a pinch of chilli powder, ground cumin and seasoning to taste.

Variations

Use 30-45 ml (2-3 tbsp) ready-prepared curry powder if preferred to save a little time. Use leeks in place of onions.

Cook's tip

The curry sauce will freeze well for up to 3 months, so it is well worthwhile making double the quantity.

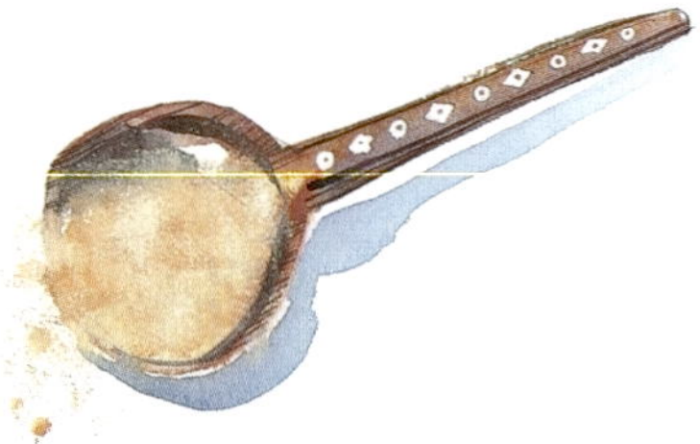

Lentil Moussaka

Sample the flavours of the Greek islands with this classic, popular dish.

Preparation time: 1 hour • Cooking time: 40 minutes • Serves: 4-6

Ingredients

140 g (5 oz) whole green lentils
1 large aubergine, sliced
60-75 ml (4-5 tbsp) olive oil
1 large onion, chopped
1 clove garlic, crushed
1 large carrot, diced
4 sticks celery, finely chopped
5-10 ml (1-2 tsp) dried mixed herbs
400-g (14-oz) can chopped tomatoes
10 ml (2 tsp) shoyu (Japanese soy sauce)
Freshly ground black pepper, to taste
2 medium potatoes, cooked and sliced
2 large tomatoes, sliced

For the sauce

55 g (2 oz) vegetable margarine
55 g (2 oz) brown rice flour
425 ml (¾ pint) milk
1 large egg, separated
55 g (2 oz) grated vegetarian Cheddar cheese
5 ml (1 tsp) ground nutmeg
Fresh herb sprigs, to garnish

Method

1
Cook the lentils in plenty of water in a saucepan until soft. Drain and reserve the liquid and lentils separately.

2
Meanwhile, fry the aubergine in the oil in a pan until lightly browned. Drain well and set aside.

3
Sauté the onion, garlic, carrot, celery and a little of the lentil stock in a pan. Simmer with the lid on until just tender, stirring occasionally.

4
Add the lentils, mixed herbs and canned tomatoes. Simmer gently for 3-4 minutes. Season with shoyu and pepper.

5
Place a layer of the lentil mixture in a large casserole dish and cover with half the aubergine slices.

6
Cover the aubergine slices with half the potato slices and all the tomato slices. Repeat with the remaining lentils, aubergines and potatoes.

7
For the sauce, melt the margarine in a saucepan, remove from the heat and stir in the flour to form a roux. Add the milk gradually, blending well so that the sauce is smooth.

8
Return to the heat and stir continuously until the sauce thickens.

9
Remove the pan from the heat and cool slightly. Add the egg yolk, stir in the cheese and add the nutmeg.

10
Whisk the egg white in a bowl until stiff, then carefully fold into the sauce.

11
Pour the sauce over the moussaka, covering the dish completely. Bake in a preheated oven at 180°C/350°F/Gas Mark 4 for about 40 minutes, until the top is golden brown and puffy. Serve hot, garnished with fresh herb sprigs.

Serving suggestion

Serve with a crunchy green salad.

Variations

Use whole brown lentils in place of green. Use sweet potatoes in place of standard potatoes.

Vegetarian Paella

This easy-to-prepare dish is full of colour and interesting texture.

Preparation time: 15 minutes • Cooking time: 1 hour • Serves: 4-6

Ingredients

60 ml (4 tbsp) olive oil
1 large onion, chopped
2 cloves garlic, crushed
2.5 ml (1/2 tsp) paprika
350 g (12 oz) long-grain brown rice
850 ml (1 1/2 pints) vegetable stock
175 ml (6 fl oz) dry white wine
400-g (14-oz) can tomatoes, plus juice, chopped
15 ml (1 tbsp) tomato purée
2.5 ml (1/2 tsp) dried tarragon
5 ml (1 tsp) dried basil
5 ml (1 tsp) dried oregano
1 red pepper, seeded and roughly chopped
1 green pepper, seeded and roughly chopped
3 sticks celery, finely chopped
225 g (8 oz) mushrooms, sliced
55 g (2 oz) mangetout, topped, tailed and cut in half
115 g (4 oz) frozen peas
55 g (2 oz) cashew nut pieces
Salt and freshly ground black pepper
Chopped fresh parsley, lemon wedges and olives, to garnish

Method

1
Heat the oil in a saucepan or paella pan and fry the onion and garlic until soft.

2
Add the paprika and rice and continue to cook for 4-5 minutes, until the rice is transparent, stirring occasionally.

3
Add the stock, wine, tomatoes, tomato purée and herbs and simmer for 10-15 minutes, stirring occasionally.

4
Add the peppers, celery, mushrooms and mangetout and continue to cook for a further 30 minutes, until the rice is cooked, stirring occasionally. Add a little extra stock, if necessary.

5
Add the peas, cashew nuts and seasoning to taste.

6
Cook until the peas are cooked, then place on a large heated serving dish.

7
Sprinkle the parsley over the top and garnish with lemon wedges and olives. Serve.

Serving suggestion

Serve with crusty French bread and a mixed dark leaf salad.

Variations

Use a mixture of brown and wild rice for a change. Use unsweetened apple juice in place of white wine. Use fresh wild mushrooms in place of cultivated mushrooms.

Cook's tip

To prepare in advance, undercook slightly, add a little more stock or water and reheat. Do not add the peas until just before serving, otherwise they will lose their colour.

Beany Lasagne

This tasty lasagne is suitable for a family meal or for entertaining friends.

Preparation time: 35 minutes • Cooking time: 35 minutes • Serves: 4-6

Ingredients

8 sheets wholemeal lasagne
1 large onion, finely chopped
15 ml (1 tbsp) vegetable oil
Salt
1-2 cloves garlic, crushed
225 g (8 oz) cooked aduki beans
1 green pepper, seeded and chopped
400-g (14-oz) can chopped tomatoes
15 ml (1 tbsp) tomato purée
5 ml (1 tsp) dried basil
5 ml (1 tsp) dried oregano
Shoyu (Japanese soy sauce) or salt
Freshly ground black pepper

For the sauce

25 g (1 oz) vegetable margarine or butter
25 g (1 oz) plain wholemeal flour
425 ml (3/4 pint) cold dairy or soya milk
55 g (2 oz) vegetarian Cheddar cheese, grated (optional)
Fresh herbs sprigs, to garnish

Method

1
Cook the lasagne in a large pan of boiling salted water for 8-10 minutes, until al dente. Drain well and drape over a cooling rack or the sides of a colander to cool and prevent sticking together.

2
Meanwhile, in a pan, soften the onion in the oil, sprinkling with a little salt to draw out the juice, then add the garlic.

3
Add the beans, pepper, tomatoes, tomato purée and dried herbs and stir to mix.

4
Simmer for about 10 minutes, or until the vegetables are tender, stirring occasionally.

5
Stir in the shoyu and season to taste.

6
Meanwhile, for the sauce, combine the margarine or butter, flour and milk in a pan. Gradually bring to the boil, whisking continuously.

7
When thickened, allow to simmer, partly covered, for about 6 minutes, stirring frequently.

8
Stir the cheese, if using, into the sauce and season.

9
Layer the lasagne in a greased dish in the following order: half the bean mix, half the pasta, the remainder of the bean mix, then the remainder of the pasta. Top with the sauce.

10
Bake in a preheated oven at 180°C/350°F/Gas Mark 4 for about 35 minutes, or until golden brown and bubbling.

11
Serve in the dish in which it has been cooked and garnish with fresh herb sprigs.

Serving suggestion

Serve with a green salad and crusty fresh bread.

Variations

Use lasagne verde in place of wholemeal lasagne. Use other cooked beans such as black-eye or flageolet in place of aduki beans.

Carrot and Cashew Nut Roast

A delicious dish to serve hot, but the full flavour of the caraway seeds and lemon are more prominent when the roast is served cold.

Preparation time: 20 minutes • Cooking time: 1 hour 10 minutes • Serves: 6

Ingredients

1 medium onion, chopped
1-2 cloves garlic, crushed
15 ml (1 tbsp) olive or sunflower oil
450 g (1 lb) carrots, cooked and mashed
225 g (8 oz) cashew nuts, ground
115 g (4 oz) fresh wholemeal breadcrumbs
15 ml (1 tbsp) light tahini
7.5 ml (1½ tsp) caraway seeds
5 ml (1 tsp) yeast extract
Juice of ½ lemon
75 ml (2½ fl oz) stock from the carrots or water
Salt and freshly ground black pepper
Fresh parsley sprigs and pepper slices, to garnish

Method

1
In a pan, fry the onion and garlic in the oil until soft, stirring occasionally. Remove from the heat.

2
In a bowl, mix together the onion and garlic with all the remaining ingredients, except the garnish, and season to taste with salt and pepper. Mix well.

3
Place the mixture in a greased 900-g (2-lb) loaf tin and level the surface.

4
Cover with foil and bake in a preheated oven at 180°C/350°F/Gas Mark 4 for 1 hour.

5
Remove the foil and bake for a further 10 minutes.

6
Leave to stand in the baking tin for at least 10 minutes before turning out.

7
Turn out onto a serving plate and serve in slices, garnished with fresh parsley sprigs and pepper slices.

Serving suggestions

Serve hot with roast potatoes and a green vegetable such as cabbage, or cold with a mixed green salad and garlic or herb-flavoured bread.

Variations

Use swede, parsnips or a mixture of root vegetables in place of carrots. Use cumin seeds in place of caraway seeds. Use almonds or hazelnuts in place of cashew nuts.

Cook's tip

This loaf can be frozen at the end of step 3. When required, remove from the freezer and thaw overnight in the refrigerator, then continue from step 4. Alternatively, freeze at the end of step 6.

Potato and Courgette Gratin

A quick and easy yet rich and flavoursome baked dish.

Preparation time: 10 minutes • Cooking time: 20-25 minutes • Serves: 2

Ingredients

250 g (9 oz) cooked potatoes, sliced

250 g (9 oz) courgettes, sliced

2 cloves garlic, crushed

250 ml (7 fl oz) double cream

Freshly ground sea salt and black pepper

15-30 ml (1-2 tbsp) chopped fresh tarragon

50 g (1¾ oz) grated vegetarian Emmenthal cheese

A knob of butter

Method

1
Lay the potato and courgette slices overlapping in a greased soufflé dish.

2
In a bowl, mix the crushed garlic with the cream. Season to taste with salt and pepper.

3
Stir in the chopped tarragon, then pour the mixture evenly over the vegetables.

4
Sprinkle over the grated cheese and dot with the butter.

5
Bake in a preheated oven at 220°C/425°F/Gas Mark 7 for 20-25 minutes, until cooked and golden brown. Serve hot.

Serving suggestion

Serve with a crisp green salad and crusty French bread or ciabatta.

Variations

Use sweet potatoes in place of standard potatoes. Use mushrooms in place of courgettes. Use vegetarian Cheddar cheese in place of Emmenthal. Use fresh basil or parsley in place of tarragon.

Cucumber in a Creamy Dill Sauce

Fresh dill provides the perfect flavouring for cucumber in this unusual vegetable side dish.

Preparation time: 15 minutes • Cooking time: 20 minutes • Serves: 4-6

Ingredients

2-3 cucumbers, weighing about 800 g (1 lb 12 oz) in total

15 ml (1 tbsp) butter

1 bunch of spring onions, trimmed and sliced

1 red pepper, seeded and cut into small pieces

Finely grated rind and juice of 1 lemon

Salt and white pepper

120 ml (8 tbsp) double cream

30 ml (2 tbsp) dry white wine

15-30 ml (1-2 tbsp) chopped fresh dill

Method

1
Remove and discard the skin from the cucumbers, then cut in half lengthways. Remove and discard the seeds with a spoon and cut the flesh into slices about 1-cm (½-in) thick.

2
Melt the butter in a pan, add the spring onions and cook for 5 minutes, until softened, stirring occasionally.

3
Add the cucumber and cook gently for 3 minutes, stirring occasionally.

4
Add the pepper to the cucumber mixture and cook for 5 minutes, until softened, stirring occasionally.

5
Add the lemon rind and juice and salt and pepper to taste. Cover the pan and cook gently for a further 7 minutes, stirring occasionally.

6
Stir in the cream, then cook briefly over a higher heat before adding the wine. Sprinkle with chopped dill before serving. Serve hot.

Serving suggestions

Serve with cheese-topped oven-baked potatoes and fresh crusty bread or grilled polenta.

Variations

Use fresh mint in place of dill. Use lime rind and juice in place of lemon. Use crème fraîche in place of cream.

Garlic Baby New Potatoes

These delectable pan-fried potatoes flavoured with garlic, fresh thyme and spring onions make a great snack or accompaniment.

Preparation time: 10 minutes • Cooking time: 20-25 minutes • Serves: 2-4

Ingredients

500 g (1 lb 2 oz) baby new potatoes
1 bunch of spring onions
30 ml (2 tbsp) olive oil
10 small fresh cloves garlic
Salt and freshly ground black pepper
15 ml (1 tbsp) finely chopped fresh thyme

Method

1
Scrub the potatoes with a brush. Remove and discard the roots and darker green foliage from the spring onions and cut in half lengthways.

2
Heat the oil in a pan, add the potatoes and cook until evenly lightly browned all over, stirring frequently.

3
Add the spring onions and garlic and cook for about 5 minutes, stirring occasionally.

4
Season with salt and pepper and sprinkle with the thyme.

5
Add a little water and cook for a further 10-15 minutes, until the potatoes are cooked and tender, stirring occasionally. Serve hot.

Serving suggestion

Serve as an accompaniment to grilled or roast mixed vegetables, such as aubergines, peppers and courgettes.

Variations

Use sesame oil in place of olive oil. Use fresh marjoram, oregano or chives in place of thyme.

Cook's tip

Do not let the garlic brown too much, or it will taste bitter.

Tabouleh

This is a traditional salad from the Middle East. The main ingredient is bulgur, which is partially cooked cracked wheat and only needs soaking for a short while before it is ready to eat.

Preparation time: 20 minutes, plus standing time • Serves: 6

Ingredients

175-200 g (6-7 oz) bulgur wheat

5 ml (1 tsp) salt

450 g (1 lb) tomatoes, chopped

½ cucumber, diced

3-4 spring onions, chopped

Fresh mint sprigs, to garnish

For the dressing

50 ml (2 fl oz) olive oil

50 ml (2 fl oz) fresh lemon juice

30 ml (2 tbsp) chopped fresh mint

60 ml (4 tbsp) chopped fresh parsley

2 cloves garlic, crushed

Method

1

Mix the bulgur wheat with the salt in a bowl, pour over 350 ml (12 fl oz) water and leave for 15-20 minutes. All the water will then be absorbed.

2

Meanwhile, whisk together all the ingredients for the dressing in a small bowl, then pour over the soaked bulgur. Fold in lightly with a spoon.

3

Cover and leave for 2 hours, or overnight in the refrigerator or a cool place.

4

Add the tomatoes, cucumber and spring onions to the bulgur wheat and mix well. Serve, garnished with fresh mint sprigs.

Serving suggestions

Serve with vegetable flans, cold vegetable pies and nut roasts.

Variations

Use cooked couscous or rice in place of bulgur wheat. Use plum tomatoes in place of standard potatoes. Use walnut or hazelnut oil in place of olive oil. Use fresh lime or orange juice in place of lemon juice.

Cook's tip

A few cooked beans can be added to make this dish more substantial.

Green Pepper Salad

Serve this salad in individual dishes as a starter accompanied by crusty brown bread or as a light lunch with bread and chunks of cheese.

Preparation time: 10 minutes, plus marinating time • Serves: 4-6

Ingredients

3 medium green peppers
3 medium tomatoes
2 medium onions
85 g (3 oz) sprouted lentils
Black grapes, to garnish

For the dressing

60 ml (4 tbsp) olive oil
30 ml (2 tbsp) red wine vinegar
10 ml (2 tsp) ground cumin
2.5 ml (½ tsp) chopped fresh coriander

Method

1
Core, seed and thinly slice the peppers.

2
Slice the tomatoes and onions.

3
Arrange the peppers, tomatoes and onions alternately on a round serving dish and sprinkle the lentil sprouts over the top.

4
In a bowl, whisk all the ingredients for the dressing together thoroughly and pour over the vegetables.

5
Cover and leave to marinate for at least 1 hour at room temperature before serving.

6
Just before serving, garnish with halved black grapes and serve.

Serving suggestions
Serve with oven-baked potatoes with cheese or grilled polenta.

Variations
Use plum tomatoes in place of standard tomatoes. Use alfalfa sprouts in place of sprouted lentils. Use walnut or hazelnut oil in place of olive oil. Use ground coriander in place of cumin.

Cook's tips
Make sure you only sprout whole lentils – red split lentils will not sprout. You can prepare this salad in advance and refrigerate until required, but remove from the refrigerator 30 minutes before serving.

Broccoli and Cauliflower Salad

A simple crisp vegetable salad served with a creamy Greek yogurt dressing.

Preparation time: 10 minutes • Serves: 4

Ingredients

1 red pepper

280 g (10 oz) broccoli

280 g (10 oz) cauliflower

15 ml (1 tbsp) toasted flaked almonds

For the dressing

60 ml (4 tbsp) Greek yogurt

30 ml (2 tbsp) fresh lemon juice

30 ml (2 tbsp) olive oil

Salt and freshly ground black pepper

A pinch of ground nutmeg

Method

1
Seed the pepper and cut into matchstick pieces. Set aside.

2
Trim the broccoli and cauliflower and break into small florets.

3
Place the pepper, broccoli and cauliflower in a mixing bowl.

4
For the dressing, combine the yogurt, lemon juice, oil, salt and pepper and nutmeg in a clean screw-top jar and shake well.

5
Pour the dressing over the salad and toss together to mix well.

6
Divide the mixture between 4 individual serving plates or bowls and garnish with the almond flakes. Serve.

Serving suggestions

Serve with crackers, oatcakes or crusty fresh bread.

Variations

Omit the nutmeg from the dressing and add a few chopped fresh herbs. Use cherry tomatoes or button mushrooms in place of cauliflower. Use fresh lime juice in place of lemon juice.

Mount Carmel Salad

Serve this crunchy salad as an accompaniment to a hot main dish or as a tasty snack.

Preparation time: 10 minutes • Serves: 4-6

Ingredients

115 g (4 oz) carrots, peeled

1 green pepper

55 g (2 oz) fresh apricots

15 ml (1 tbsp) sesame seeds

225 g (8 oz) beansprouts

60 ml (4 tbsp) French dressing

30 ml (2 tbsp) unsweetened pineapple juice

Method

1
Cut the carrots into matchstick strips. Set aside.

2
Seed and thinly slice the pepper. Set aside.

3
Cut the apricots into slivers. Set aside.

4
Toast the sesame seeds in a dry pan over a low heat until golden brown. Remove from the heat and set aside.

5
Place the carrots, pepper, apricots and beansprouts in a serving dish.

6
Mix the French dressing with the pineapple juice in a bowl and fold into the salad.

7
Sprinkle the sesame seeds over the top and serve at once.

Serving suggestions

Serve as an accompaniment to vegetable flans or pizzas, or with fresh crusty bread.

Variations

Use pumpkin or sunflower seeds in place of sesame seeds. Use apple or orange juice in place of pineapple juice. Use courgettes in place of carrots.

Cook's tip

Use beansprouts which are at least 2.5 cm (1 in) long for this recipe.

Greek Salad

A classic and ever-appealing salad of marinated vegetables and feta cheese.

Preparation time: 15 minutes, plus marinating time • Cooking time: 5-10 minutes • Serves: 4

Ingredients

60 ml (4 tbsp) olive oil
4 small courgettes, sliced
15 ml (1 tbsp) finely chopped fresh dill
30 ml (2 tbsp) walnut oil
30 ml (2 tbsp) fresh lemon juice
15 ml (1 tbsp) tarragon vinegar
Salt and freshly ground black pepper, to taste
Sugar, to taste
4 large tomatoes, skinned
1 red pepper, seeded
1 green pepper, seeded
2 onions
250 g (9 oz) feta cheese, crumbled
30 ml (2 tbsp) finely chopped fresh parsley
5 ml (1 tsp) finely chopped fresh mint or lemon balm
1 lettuce

Method

1
Heat the olive oil in a pan and cook the courgettes until lightly browned all over, stirring occasionally. Sprinkle with dill.

2
Pour the cooking liquid into a bowl and add the walnut oil, lemon juice, vinegar, pepper and salt and sugar. Mix well and set aside.

3
Slice the tomatoes, slice the peppers into strips, then slice the onions into rings.

4
Add the tomatoes, peppers and onions to the marinade and mix well.

5
Add the courgette slices, feta and herbs to the marinade and mix all the ingredients together thoroughly.

6
Cover and leave to marinate in the refrigerator for about 1 hour.

7
Before serving, shred the lettuce leaves, then mix with the salad. Serve immediately.

Servings suggestions

Serve with ciabatta or warmed pitta bread.

Variations

Use red onions in place of standard onions. Use hazelnut or olive oil in place of walnut oil. Use other herb-flavoured vinegars in place of tarragon vinegar. Use vegetarian Cheddar or Mozzarella cheese in place of feta cheese.

Mixed Seed Bread Rolls

These seed-topped bread rolls make a delicious snack at any time of the day. Serve freshly baked, warm or cold.

Preparation time: 20 minutes, plus kneading and rising time • Cooking time: 15-20 minutes • Makes: about 12

Ingredients

500 g (1 lb 2 oz) strong white flour

125 ml (4 fl oz) lukewarm milk

A large pinch of sugar

25 g (1 oz) fresh yeast

100 g (3½ oz) butter, at room temperature

2 medium eggs, plus 2 egg yolks

15 ml (1 tbsp) salt

30-45 ml (2-3 tbsp) olive oil

15 ml (1 tbsp) caraway seeds

15 ml (1 tbsp) coarse sea salt

15 ml (1 tbsp) coriander seeds

Method

1
Sift the flour into a bowl. Add the milk, stir in the sugar, then crumble the yeast into the mixture.

2
Mix to a smooth dough, knead gently, then leave to rise for 10-15 minutes.

3
Add the butter, 2 whole eggs, salt and 15-30 ml (1-2 tbsp) of the oil to the dough and work into the dough until well mixed and smooth.

4
Cover the dough and set aside in a warm place for about 30 minutes to rise.

5
Knead the dough once more and set aside for a further 30 minutes.

6
Divide the dough into about 12 small balls, then roll each out on a lightly floured work surface.

7
Grease a baking sheet with the remaining oil. Place the dough balls on the baking sheet and flatten each one out slightly.

8
In a bowl, beat the egg yolks with 60 ml (4 tbsp) water and brush the dough balls with the mixture.

9
Sprinkle the dough balls with caraway seeds, salt and coriander seeds. Leave for a further 10 minutes to rise.

10
Bake in a preheated oven at 180°C/350°F/Gas Mark 7 for 15-20 minutes, until risen, cooked and golden brown. Serve warm or cold.

Serving suggestions

Serve spread with butter, savoury spread or vegetarian paté.

Variations

Use wholemeal flour or a mixture of white and wholemeal flour in place of all white flour. Use cumin, poppy or sesame seeds in place of caraway seeds.

Cook's tip

Use a mixer with a dough hook attachment to mix and knead the bread dough, to save a little time and effort.

Autumn Loaf

This potato bread is ideal served freshly baked and still warm for a welcome snack.

Preparation time: 40 minutes, plus kneading and rising times • Cooking time: 40 -50 minutes • Makes: 2 x 450 g (1 lb) loaves

Ingredients

500 g (1 lb 2 oz) floury potatoes
40 g (1½ oz) fresh yeast, crumbled
500 g (1 lb 2 oz) plain strong wholemeal flour
200 ml (7 fl oz) lukewarm milk
45 ml (3 tbsp) butter, softened
5 ml (1 tsp) sea salt
1 eating apple
150 g (5½ oz) sunflower seeds

Method

1
Wash the potatoes, then cook in a large saucepan of lightly salted, boiling water for about 20 minutes, until tender.

2
Peel the potatoes while they are still hot, then mash well. Set aside.

3
Dissolve the yeast in 30-45 ml (2-3 tbsp) lukewarm water in a bowl. Mix the yeast with the flour in a large bowl, then add the milk, a further 200 ml (7 fl oz) lukewarm water and the butter. Add the salt, then knead well to form a smooth dough.

4
Peel and core the apple, then finely grate.

5
Heat all but 30 ml (2 tbsp) of the sunflower seeds in a pan without any oil or fat for 5 minutes, then knead into the dough, together with the mashed potatoes and grated apple.

6
Place the dough in a bowl, cover and set aside in a warm place for about 1½ hours to rise.

7
Grease two 450 g (1 lb) loaf tins, divide the dough equally between them, then sprinkle with the remaining 30 ml (2 tbsp) sunflower seeds and leave to rise in a warm place for a further 40 minutes.

8
Bake in a preheated oven at 220°C/425°F/Gas Mark 7 for about 40-50 minutes, until cooked. When cooked, turn the bread out of the tins on its side and place on a wire rack to cool. Serve in slices.

Serving suggestions
Serve in slices, warm or cold, spread with a little butter, vegetable margarine or savoury vegetable paté.

Variations
Use sweet potatoes in place of standard potatoes. Use pumpkin, sesame or poppy seeds in place of sunflower seeds. Use 1 pear in place of the apple.

Almond and Carrot Bread

A moist, flavourful bread, combining nuts, carrots, sultanas and honey.

Preparation time: 25 minutes, plus kneading and rising time • Cooking time: 50-55 minutes • Makes: 12-16 slices

Ingredients

300 g (10½ oz) carrots
15-30 ml (1-2 tbsp) lemon juice
500 g (1 lb 2 oz) strong white flour
1 sachet dried yeast
45 ml (3 tbsp) flaked wholewheat grains
100 g (3½ oz) ground almonds
5 ml (1 tsp) sea salt
45 ml (3 tbsp) honey
100 g (3½ oz) butter, softened
1 medium egg, beaten
150 g (5½ oz) sultanas
40 g (1½ oz) blanched almonds

Method

1
Grate the carrots into a bowl and sprinkle with lemon juice. Set aside.

2
In a separate bowl, mix the flour thoroughly with the yeast, then add the flaked grains, ground almonds, salt, honey, butter, egg and 100 ml (3½ fl oz) lukewarm water and work in the ingredients to form a smooth dough.

3
Knead the dough for about 5 minutes. While kneading, add the grated carrot a little at a time.

4
Add the sultanas and knead well.

5
Place the dough in a bowl, cover and leave in a warm place until risen to about double its original volume. Knead once more on a lightly floured work surface.

6
Sprinkle half the blanched almonds over the base of a greased soufflé dish and place the dough on top. Sprinkle the remaining almonds over the top of the dough.

7
Press the dough gently down into the dish, then cover and leave in a warm place once again until risen to double its volume.

8
Bake in a preheated oven at 200°C/400°F/Gas Mark 6 for 50-55 minutes, until cooked.

9
Turn out onto a wire rack to cool and serve in slices.

Serving suggestions

Serve warm or cold in slices, spread with butter, vegetable margarine, honey or preserve.

Variations

Use courgettes in place of carrots. Use ground and blanched hazelnuts in place of almonds. Use chopped ready-to-eat dried apricots in place of sultanas.

Muesli Cookies

These fruit and nut cookies with a honey coating make a healthy and satisfying treat or snack whenever you feel hungry.

Preparation time: 25 minutes, plus kneading and resting time • Cooking time: 20-25 minutes • Makes: about 40

Ingredients

125 g (4½ oz) coarse oatmeal
100 g (3½ oz) stoned prunes
100 g (3½ oz) sultanas
100 g (3½ oz) hazelnuts
100 g (3½ oz) butter
200 g (7 oz) golden syrup
A pinch of sea salt
Finely grated rind of 1 lemon
125 ml (4 fl oz) mineral water
125 g (4½ oz) crumbled fresh yeast
125 g (4½ oz) strong white flour
30 ml (2 tbsp) honey

Method

1
Cook the oatmeal in a pan without oil or fat until golden, stirring frequently. Remove from the heat and set aside to cool.

2
Finely chop the prunes, sultanas and hazelnuts.

3
Heat the butter and syrup in a pan until melted, remove from the heat and set aside to cool.

4
Add salt and the lemon rind to the mineral water in a jug and mix with the yeast.

5
Place the flour in a bowl, add the chopped fruit and nuts, the butter and syrup mixture and the oatmeal and yeast mixture. Knead together thoroughly to form a smooth dough.

6
Cover and leave the dough overnight in the refrigerator.

7
Using 2 spoons, place small balls of the dough on baking sheets lined with greaseproof or non-stick baking paper.

8
Bake in a preheated oven at 200°C/400°F/Gas Mark 6 for 20-25 minutes, until golden brown and cooked.

9
Transfer to a wire rack to cool.

10
Mix the honey with 30 ml (2 tbsp) boiling water in a bowl and brush the cooled cookies with the honey mixture. Leave to dry, then serve.

Serving suggestion
Serve as a treat or snack with a glass of sparkling apple juice.

Variations
Use ready-to-eat dried pears or peaches or figs in place of prunes. Use almonds or walnuts in place of hazelnuts. Use lime rind in place of lemon rind.

Cook's tip
A quick and easy way to chop dried fruit such as prunes is to snip them into pieces using a clean pair of kitchen scissors.

Chocolate and Almond Biscuits

These tempting little crunchy biscuits are a real treat. Serve as an after-dinner sweetmeat.

Preparation time: 40 minutes, plus overnight chilling time • Cooking time: 12-15 minutes • Makes: about 50

Ingredients

500 g (1 lb 2 oz) plain white flour

10 ml (2 tsp) baking powder

150 g (5½ oz) caster sugar, plus 15 ml (1 tbsp)

15 g (½ oz) vanilla sugar

A pinch of salt

1 large egg, beaten

350 g (12 oz) cold butter, diced

40 g (1½ oz) cocoa powder, sifted

15 ml (1 tbsp) milk or rum

100 g (3½ oz) coarsely chopped blanched almonds

A little egg white, for brushing

Method

1
Sift the flour and baking powder into a bowl and mix well.

2
Make a well in the centre and add the 150 g (5½ oz) sugar, vanilla sugar, salt and egg and mix well.

3
Rub in the butter a little at a time and gradually knead the mixture to form a smooth dough.

4
Set aside about one third of the dough.

5
Add the cocoa powder, the remaining 15 ml (1 tbsp) caster sugar, milk or rum and the chopped almonds to the remaining dough, kneading well.

6
Form the dough into 4 rectangular sausage shapes about 31 cm (12½ in) long, 3 cm (1¼ in) wide and about 1.5 cm (⅝ in) thick.

7
Roll out the reserved dough to about 44 cm (17½ in) by 31 cm (12½ in) and cut into 4 strips, each about 11 cm (4¼ in) by 31 cm (12½ in).

8
Brush the dough with a little egg white and place one sausage of almond-flavoured dough on each piece of plain dough and wrap the plain dough around the flavoured dough, enclosing it completely.

9
Wrap each 'loaf' in aluminium foil and chill overnight in the refrigerator.

10
Unwrap the loaves, cut into 1-cm (½-in) slices and place on greased baking trays covered with greaseproof or non-stick baking paper.

11
Bake in a preheated oven at 200°C/400°F/Gas Mark 6 for 12-15 minutes, until cooked.

12
Transfer to a wire rack to cool before serving.

Serving suggestions

Serve with a glass of dessert wine or freshly squeezed fruit juice.

Variations

Use half white and half wholemeal flour in place of all white flour. Use hazelnuts or pecan nuts in place of almonds.

Cook's tip

Store the cold cooked cookies in an airtight container to keep them as fresh as possible.

Choc-Oat Slices

These delicious, wholesome snacks are perfect for the lunch box or a children's party.

Preparation time: 10 minutes • Cooking time: 25-30 minutes • Makes: 12 slices

Ingredients

115 g (4 oz) carob bar	*225 g (8 oz) porridge oats*
115 g (4 oz) hard vegetable margarine	*115 g (4 oz) sultanas*
15 ml (1 tbsp) clear honey	*55 g (2 oz) desiccated coconut*

Method

1
Break the carob into a pan and add the margarine and honey.

2
Melt over a very low heat and stir until all the ingredients have melted and blended.

3
Remove from the heat and stir in the oats, sultanas and coconut.

4
Spread the mixture evenly into a greased shallow, rectangular 28 x 18 cm (11 x 7 in) baking tin and bake in a preheated oven at 180°C/350°F/Gas Mark 4 for 25-30 minutes.

5
Cool slightly, then mark into slices. Place on a wire rack to cool.

6
When completely cold, remove from the tin and store in an airtight container.

Serving suggestion
Serve with a glass of freshly squeezed orange juice.

Cook's tip
Wrapped in foil or sealed in a container, these slices freeze well for up to 3 months.

Brandied Oranges with Peach and Mango Cream

An attractive dessert which tastes as good as it looks.

Preparation time: 20 minutes, plus chilling time • Cooking time: 2 minutes • Serves: 4

Ingredients

6 large jaffa oranges

45 ml (3 tbsp) brandy

2 mangoes, peeled, stoned and cut into chunks

4 small ripe peaches, peeled, stoned and roughly chopped

45 ml (3 tbsp) double cream

Method

1
Finely pare the zest from 3 of the oranges and boil the zest in a little water in a pan for 2 minutes.

2
Remove from the heat, drain and cool.

3
Peel the oranges using a sharp knife, making sure that all the pith is removed.

4
Thinly slice the oranges, arrange in a serving dish and sprinkle the zest over the top.

5
Sprinkle the brandy over the oranges, cover and refrigerate for about 1 hour.

6
Place the mangoes and peaches in a food processor or blender and blend until smooth. Place in a bowl.

7
Stir in the cream, cover and refrigerate until required.

8
Serve the oranges with the peach and mango cream alongside.

Serving suggestion

Serve with wafer or sponge finger biscuits.

Variations

Use Greek yogurt or crème fraîche in place of double cream. Use nectarines in place of peaches.
Use pink or ruby grapefruit in place of oranges.

Cook's tip

Use a zester to remove the zest from the oranges.

Almond Steamed Pudding

A deliciously light and moist steamed sponge pudding – ideal for a family dessert.

Preparation time: 15 minutes • Cooking time: 1-1½ hours • Serves: 4-6

Ingredients

100 g (3½ oz) butter, softened

100 g (3½ oz) caster sugar

15 g (½ oz) vanilla sugar

3 medium eggs

A pinch of salt

2 drops of almond essence

50 g (1¾ oz) almonds or hazelnuts, chopped

150 g (5½ oz) plain flour, sifted

50 g (1¾ oz) cornflour

10 ml (2 tsp) baking powder, sifted

45 ml (3 tbsp) milk

A little flour, for dusting

Method

1

Beat the butter in a bowl until creamy, then gradually beat in the caster sugar, vanilla sugar, eggs, salt and almond essence.

2

Stir in the nuts, then fold in the flour, cornflour and baking powder. Stir in the milk and mix well.

3

Grease a pudding basin and dust with a little flour.

4

Spoon the almond mixture into the bowl and level the surface.

5

Cover with greased greaseproof paper and secure with string.

6

Steam in a steamer over a pan of boiling water for 1-1½ hours, or until risen and cooked.

7

Turn out onto a warmed serving plate and serve immediately.

Serving suggestions

Serve with chocolate sauce or zabaglione.

Variations

Use vanilla essence in place of almond essence. Use currants or sultanas in place of nuts.
Use half white and half wholemeal flour in place of all white flour.

Fruit Salad Trifle

A sumptuous trifle of mixed fruits and nuts with a light carob sponge base and a cream-yogurt topping – ideal for entertaining.

Preparation time: 30 minutes, plus cooling and chilling time • Cooking time: 20 minutes • Serves: 6

Ingredients

For the carob sponge

115 g (4 oz) soft vegetable margarine

85 g (3 oz) light muscovado sugar, finely ground

2 medium eggs

85 g (3 oz) plain wholemeal flour, sifted

25 g (1 oz) carob powder

7.5 ml (1½ tsp) baking powder

For the trifle

90 ml (6 tbsp) apple juice

15-30 ml (1-2 tbsp) apricot or banana liqueur (optional)

2 crisp eating apples, cored and chopped but not peeled

1 large banana, sliced

2 oranges, segmented and roughly chopped

Half a pineapple, cored and diced

A few grapes, halved and seeded

55 g (2 oz) fresh dates, stoned and chopped

55 g (2 oz) hazelnuts, chopped

115 g (4 oz) whipping cream

115 g (4 oz) Greek yogurt

Orange segments, pineapple cubes and carob chips, to decorate

Method

1
Cream the margarine and sugar together in a bowl until pale and fluffy.

2
Beat in the eggs one at a time, then carefully fold in the flour, carob powder and baking powder.

3
Turn into 2 greased 18-cm (7-in) sponge or flan tins and level the surfaces. Bake in a preheated oven at 180°C/350°F/Gas Mark 4 for about 20 minutes, until golden brown and risen.

4
Turn out onto a wire rack to cool. Set aside.

5
Place one of the carob sponges in a trifle bowl and pour the apple juice over the sponge. Set aside for 30 minutes.

6
Drizzle over the liqueur, if using, then arrange the prepared fruits and nuts over the sponge, covering it completely.

7
In a bowl, whip the cream until stiff, then fold in the yogurt.

8
Spread evenly over the fruit, covering it completely.

9
With the back of a fork, trace from the rim of the bowl into the centre, making a lined effect. Chill before serving. Decorate with orange segments, pineapple cubes and carob chips and serve.

Serving suggestion

Trifle is best served on its own or with a little extra cream or yogurt.

Variations

Use your own choice of fresh prepared fruit for this trifle. Use cocoa powder in place of carob powder. Use plain white flour in place of wholemeal flour. Use almonds or pistachio nuts in place of hazelnuts.

Cook's tip

Since this recipes makes two halves of sponge and only one is needed for the trifle, the other half can be frozen or used on a subsequent occasion.

Cashew Ice Cream

For special occasions, just add 15 ml (1 tbsp) of rum for an even more impressive ice cream.

Preparation time: 10 minutes, plus freezing time • Serves: 4

Ingredients

1 large very ripe banana, roughly chopped
115 g (4 oz) finely ground cashew nuts
150 ml (1/2 pint) concentrated soya milk
2.5 ml (1/2 tsp) vanilla essence
10 ml (2 tsp) clear honey
2 rings unsweetened canned pineapple, diced

Method

1
Place all the ingredients, apart from the pineapple, in a food processor or blender and blend until smooth and well mixed.

2
Add the pineapple and blend briefly to mix.

3
Place the mixture in a shallow freezerproof container, cover and freeze for about 2 hours, or until mushy in consistency.

4
Spoon into a chilled bowl and mash with a fork to break down the ice crystals.

5
Return the mixture to the container, cover and freeze until firm.

6
Transfer to the refrigerator for about 30 minutes before serving, to allow the ice cream to soften a little.

7
Serve in scoops.

Serving suggestions

Serve with strawberries or fresh fruit salad.

Variations

Use hazelnuts, almonds or pistachio nuts in place of cashew nuts. Use maple syrup in place of honey.
Use almond essence in place of vanilla essence.

Kompot

This classic Middle Eastern dish is simple to prepare and can be made well in advance.

Preparation time: 15 minutes, plus standing time • Serves: 6-8

Ingredients

225 g (8 oz) dried prunes

225 g (8 oz) dried apricots

115 g (4 oz) dried figs

115 g (4 oz) raisins

115 g (4 oz) blanched almonds

55 g (2 oz) pine nuts

5 ml (1 tsp) ground cinnamon

1.25 ml (1/4 tsp) ground nutmeg

115 g (4 oz) light soft brown sugar

15 ml (1 tbsp) rosewater

Finely grated rind and juice of 1 orange

Method

1
Stone the prunes and roughly chop.

2
Halve the apricots and quarter the figs.

3
Place all the fruit in a large bowl and add the remaining ingredients. Stir well to mix.

4
Cover with cold water and stir well.

5
Cover and keep in a cool place for 1-2 days, stirring a couple of times each day.

6
Before serving, mix again thoroughly and spoon into bowls to serve.

Serving suggestion

Place the mixture in glass serving dishes and serve with a swirl of yogurt or cream.

Variations

Other dried fruits can be used, but keep to the same quantities. Use pistachio nuts in place of blanched almonds.

Cook's tip

After 24 hours the liquid in which the kompot is soaking will become very thick and syrupy. If you need to add more liquid, add a little orange juice.

Mixed Fruit Tart

This appealing tart makes a wonderful summertime dessert for family or friends to enjoy.

Preparation time: 25 minutes • Cooking time: 20-25 minutes • Serves: 8-10

Ingredients

For the pastry

100 g (3½ oz) plain white flour

100 g (3½ oz) buckwheat flour

A pinch of salt

15 ml (1 tbsp) honey

100 g (3½ oz) soured cream

100 g (3½ oz) butter, softened

For the filling

600-700 g (1 lb 5 oz-1 lb 9 oz) prepared soft fruit, such as strawberries, raspberries, blackberries or cooked apricots

60 ml (4 tbsp) strawberry or apricot jam

Chopped nuts, to decorate

Method

1
Sift the flours into a mixing bowl and add the salt, honey, soured cream and butter.

2
Knead the ingredients together to form a smooth dough. If the dough is sticky, place on a plate in the refrigerator for a while to rest.

3
On a lightly floured work surface, roll out the pastry to a round slightly larger than a 25-cm (10-in) fluted flan tin and use to line the tin. Trim the edges.

4
Prick a few holes in the pastry base with a fork and place on a baking tray.

5
Bake in a preheated oven at 190°C/375°F/Gas Mark 5 for 20-25 minutes, until pale golden and cooked.

6
Transfer to a wire rack to cool. Remove the flan case carefully from the tin.

7
Place the cooled flan case on a serving plate. Arrange the fruit in the flan case.

8
Heat the jam in a saucepan, stirring continuously, until runny, then brush the fruit all over with the jam.

9
Serve in slices, decorated with the chopped nuts.

Serving suggestion

Serve with maple syrup and whipped cream.

Variations

Use your own choice of fruit for this tart, such as mixed tropical fruit or autumn berries.
Use plain wholemeal flour in place of buckwheat flour.

Cook's tip

Individual tartlets may be made instead of 1 large tart. Reduce the cooking time a little for tartlets.

Index